Frogs in Clogs

A World Book Day ~~~~~ Book

Also available from Macmillan

Read Me: A Poem for Every Day of the Year
chosen by Gaby Morgan

Read Me 2: A Poem for Every Day of the Year
chosen by Gaby Morgan

**Read Me and Laugh: A Funny
Poem for Every Day of the Year**
chosen by Gaby Morgan

**The Works: Every kind of poem you will ever need
for the Literacy Hour**
chosen by Paul Cookson

Frogs in Clogs

A World Book Day Poetry Book

Chosen by Gaby Morgan

Illustrated by Jane Eccles

MACMILLAN CHILDREN'S BOOKS

For Mrs Burnett and Miss Maxie at the Alexandra Infant School, Kingston-upon-Thames. Thank you. Gaby

For Miss Goward and Ms Buck, Green Dragon Primary School, Brentford – thanks for making Year 2 so good for Theo. Jane

First published 2005
by Macmillan Children's Books
a division of Macmillan Publishers Limited
20 New Wharf Road, London N1 9RR
Basingstoke and Oxford
www.panmacmillan.com

Associated companies throughout the world

ISBN 0 330 43645 7

1 3 5 7 9 8 6 4 2

A CIP catalogue record for this book is available from the British Library.

Printed by Mackays of Chatham plc, Chatham, Kent.

Contents

under

under the autumn damp the winter chill
under the winter chill the Christmas light
under the Christmas light crocus and catkin
under the crocus and catkin the cherry blossom
under the cherry blossom the heat of summer
under the heat of summer the autumn damp

Fred Sedgwick

Shaking the Branches

(A Boy's War Poem)

I'm shaking our walnut tree,
standing in its fork,
and I can see for miles.

A farmer is ploughing
with one piebald horse.
And the crows are flying.

It's not a school day.
The sun, low on the horizon
is bright in my eyes.

My fingers are stained
with walnut juice;
my bare knees are cold.

There are apples in the barrel
and tomatoes on the sill;
and on the range, a juicy stew.

The swallows have gone
and smoke is curling
from the barley-sugar chimneys.

My parents are a hundred
miles away in a bombed city.
Churchill is on the news,
and I am standing in the fork
of a walnut tree
shaking the branches.

Gerard Benson

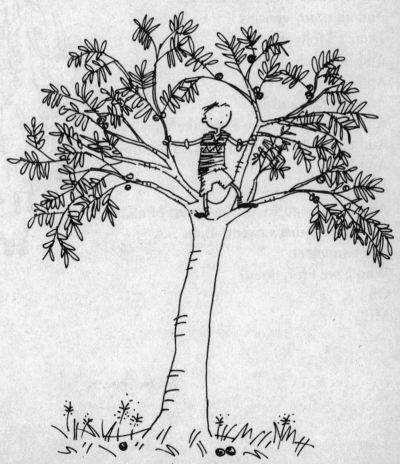

This is Our House

This is our house
Called Violet Vista
And this is Susie, my horrible sister.
Dad's my father, and Mum's my mother
And this is Barry, my baby brother.
Grandad and Gran, Grandpa and Nan,
Aunt Eliza and Great-aunt Nell
And all of my cousins live here as well –
There's Molly who's jolly
And Billie who's silly
And Jenny and Penny
And Georgie and Jilly
And Jessica June who eats cake with a spoon
And Gloria Rose with a spot on her nose
And Dolly who's tall
And Davie who's small
And Micky and Ricky the littlest of all.
All together that's twenty-three . . .
Just a moment.
Who have I forgotten?
Oh . . .
ME!

Vivian French

Missing Important Things

I didn't go to school this week
I stayed at home with Dad.
I didn't do a worksheet
and I am really rather glad.
I didn't do the number work,
I didn't do my words,
I didn't learn my spellings
And I didn't read my page.
I didn't go to school today –
we fixed the shed instead,
tied some flies and feathers
and dug the onion bed.

I saw the cat have kittens,
I climbed right up a tree,
mixed some sand and water
and held a bumblebee.
I didn't go to school all week
and I'm really not too sad –
I missed important lessons
and stayed at home with Dad.

Peter Dixon

The Super Sledging Stars

A hard, hard winter. Snow lay deep and soft.
Sledges appeared from cellar, shed and loft.
We duffled-up from head to booted feet
And, with all the traffic stilled, reclaimed our street.
We made a slide that glinted like a gun,
and sledged non-stop on our own Cresta Run.

Lying, sitting, we rattled down the slope
then dragged our sledges back on reins of rope
until we reached the top. Then off we'd go
speed-bumping down the track of hard-packed snow.
Some fell, some squealed; the hopeless ones got miffed
when they got head-stuck in a roadside drift.

All day we sledge-raced down that icy slide.
At dusk the younger ones were called inside,
but we stayed on beneath the street lights' beam
and now our slide took on a silver gleam.
Fresh snowflakes fell, enshrouding roadside cars,
as we trudged home, the super sledging stars.

Wes Magee

Child of Many Names

They call me
American Cougar
Bite-size Sugar
Spicey Ricey
Over in a Tricey
Crocodile Flutter
Snack Party Nutter
Steevee Cinch
Teeny Weeny Pinch
Down Home Dixie
Hot Fried Pixie
DJ Squidge
Empties-the-Fridge
Red, Red Rose
Little Gravel Nose
Giant Gorbelly
Witch-over-Telly
Boodie and Squean

Big Baked Bean
Crick Crack
Scratchma Back
Breakdancer Breakneck
Corporal Extendoneck
Beetroot Base
Space Face Ace
Little Grebe
Oor Wullie up the Glebe
Baby-in-Grey
Fairy Fly Away
and . . .
Seafood Sausage!

All because,
Mum and Dad say,
A loved child has many names.

John Rice

Junk Uncle

Bless Uncle Bert, untidy twit
So fond of trash, he lived in it,
In love with litter, master of mess,
How did he end up? Have a guess!
Picked up the rubbish man,
Chucked in the back of the refuse van,
Uncle Bert, to dirt attracted,
Ended his days somewhat compacted.

Andrew Fusek Peters

One Afternoon

The pitter-patter rain suddenly ceased.
Sky held its breath. Then a cloud parted

and a bright beam of warm sunlight
shot right down into the garden.

Everything started smiling. Birds struck up
a silvery chorus. And, oh, that sudden

knockout scent of velvet wallflowers
and roses with little twinkly beads of rain

like diamonds in among the petals.
Roof tiles steamed and windows gleamed.

I remember saying Let's open the garden door
and ask Summer in to tea.

Matt Simpson

These are the Hands

These are the hands that wave
These are the hands that clap
These are the hands that pray
These are the hands that tap

These are the hands that grip
These are the hands that write
These are the hands that paint
These are the hands that fight

These are the hands that hug
These are the hands that squeeze
These are the hands that point
These are the hands that tease

These are the hands that fix
These are the hands that mend
These are the hands that give
These are the hands that lend

These are the hands that take
These are the hands that poke
These are the hands that heal
These are the hands that stroke

These are the hands that hold
These are the hands that love
These are the hands of mine
That fit me like a glove

Paul Cookson

You're the Best

I love the way
You nod your head
I love the way
You walk ahead
I love the way
You sneak on my bed
I love the way
You chew the mail
I love the way
You wag your tail
You cheer me up
You never fail
Your fur's uncombed
Your coat's a mess
But I love you
And you're the best
Yes yes, yes yes –
You are the BEST!

Trevor Millum.

Mehndi* Time

(To welcome Tulika to our family)

The love of family and friends –
at *mehndi* time, at *mehndi* time –
the joy of stories and laughter –
at *mehndi* time, at *mehndi* time,
embrace me like a magic ring
as they clap their hands and sing:

> *May the new bride bring a blessing,*
> mehndi *magic mark her wedding.*
> *With designs – intricate and neat –*
> *we'll decorate her hands and feet.*

With bright lines of ochre colour –
at *mehndi* time, at *mehndi* time –
my sisters pattern loving warmth –
at *mehndi* time, at *mehndi* time.
In life my journey may be far
as I pursue my *mehndi* star.

Painted shells and lotus flowers
decorate these happy hours.
Rich mango leaves and tree of life –
love's anchors for our new-wed wife.

I will nourish tradition's fruit
at *mehndi* time, at *mehndi* time.
What memories I will cherish –
at *mehndi* time, of *mehndi* time!
Like *mehndi* bushes, cool and green,
may *mehndi* make my life serene.

Her feet are tinted coral-rose,
her hands are jewels in repose.
May her new life flow with blessing,
mehndi *magic mark her wedding.*

It's *mehndi* time, it's *mehndi* time . . .

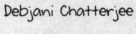

Debjani Chatterjee

mehndi: henna

If Only . . .

If only I could catch the stars
And trap them in a Kilner jar
Like silvery bright atoms.

If only I could steal a comet's tail
And tie it to a ship's sail
So that it could illuminate the sea
When the days get too dark.

If only I could snatch
A clown's mask and place it
On the twisted face of sadness.

If only I could freeze the sun
And hand out slices of frozen light
Like leaflets on a street corner
Or a deck of cold calling cards.

If only I could imprison electricity's
dazzling spark like a vein of lightning
And use it to tingle your toes.

If only I could poke a hole
Into every spiteful jibe,
As barbed as a nettle's bite.

If only I could take you home
Wrapped in an anorak of words.

I could use you in my next poem –
You'd make an explosive opening!

Pie Corbett

Big Red Boots

Big red boots, big red boots.
One of them squeaks and the other one toots.
One of them hops and the other one stamps.
Big red boots take long, wet tramps.

Big red boots, big red boots.
One of them squeaks and the other one toots.

Big red boots on busy little feet
start out shiny, clean and neat.
Big red boots, oh, yes, yes, yes,
end up muddy in a terrible mess.

Big red boots, big red boots.
One of them squeaks and the other one toots.

Boots, boots, big red boots,
squelch through mud and trample roots.
Big red boots say, 'Look! Oh gosh!
What a great puddle there . . . Yay!' SPLOSH!

Tony Mitton

The Last Bear

The last bear left, the last bear left,
The last bear left, that's me –
No other bears in all the world
To keep me company.

I climb the hills of summer,
I wade the empty streams,
I fatten up in autumn,
Winter's a cave of dreams.

My dreams are full of playing
And tumbling in a heap
With twenty other happy bears,
But then I wake from sleep,

And yawn and stretch and scratch
And search the woods once more –
No bear-scent on the north wind,
No trace of pad or paw.

The last bear left, the last bear left,
The last bear left, that's me –
No other bears in all the world
To keep me company.

Richard Edwards

Christening Gift

The gift I bestow is last but not least –
A permanent magical feast,
A path to knowledge, a key to learning
That grows with you at each year's turning,
A thousand stories for your pleasure,
Jokes and prayers in equal measure,
Conversation and songs for singing,
Poems for the joy of wild words ringing.
I grant you a life spent under its spell.
Words are my gift – use them well.

Sue Cowling

Once Upon a Time Machine

Yes, I'm caught in a time-loop,

like a circular track;

dashed into the future

– crashed, coming back

It's bad enough, being stuck

in a groove, endlessly;

the reason I'm trapped

is, I'll smash into me!

Mike Johnson

The Moon at Knowle Hill

The Moon was married last night
and nobody saw
dressed up in her ghostly dress
for the summer ball.

The stars shimmied in the sky
and danced a whirligig;
the moon vowed to be true
and lit up the corn-rigs.

She kissed the dark lips of the sky
above the summer house,
she in her pale white dress
swooned across the vast sky.

The moon was married last night,
the beautiful belle of the ball,
and nobody saw her at all
except a small girl in a navy dress

who witnessed it all.

Jackie Kay

Poem Spoken by a Cat to its Owners' Friends Who are Flat-sitting

I have eaten
the chicken
you had on the sideboard
defrosting

and which you were hoping
to roast
and serve with wine
to your friends

forgive me
I'm a cat
we have no manners
we're always like that

Matthew Sweeney

Hogging Hedgehogs

With thanks to Lewis Carroll

'Won't you trot a little faster?' said the hedgehog to the
    cat,
'The slugs are sliming frothily, there are earwigs brown
    and fat,
The snails are ripe for picking, there's a thousand grubs
    at least,
They are lurking in the compost heap, won't you come
    and join the feast?

'Will you, won't you, will you, won't you, will you join
   the feast?
Will you, won't you, will you, won't you, won't you
   join the feast?

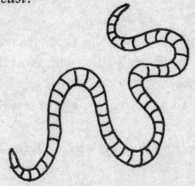

'You really can't imagine how delightful it will taste
When we bite into a beetle, or a worm, so let's make
   haste!
When he thinks of hogging maggots a hedgehog almost
   runs,
For those that get there early get the fat and juicy ones!

'Will you, *won't you, will you, won't you, will you join the feast?*
Will you, *won't you, will you, won't you, won't you join the feast?*

'I'm sure it sounds delicious,' his furry friend replied,
'So please enjoy your centipedes, with woodlice on the side,
But I've no need to join you, for I have a well-trained man,
And when I'm feeling hungry, why, he'll open up a can!

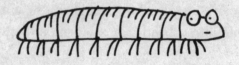

'*I will not, could not, will not, could not, will not join the feast!*
I will not, could not, will not, could not, could not join the feast!

David Orme

Boy at the Somme

'The last one there is a cow pat!'
grinned the small boy
running between the white headstones
as he began the one hundred metre dash
along the narrow strip of turf separating
Private Tom Atkins, age 18, of the Lancashire Fusiliers,
from Lieutenant Edward Hollis, age 19,
of the Seaforth Highlanders;
more than twice the distance they managed
over the same small field
that October morning eighty-seven years before
into the spitting venom of the machine guns
that killed them instantly.

Alan Durant

Seasoned Cinquains

Autumn
Tinge of henna
Crackling fires and leaves
Deep rooting tick of biding time
Digging.

Winter
Stiff morning air
Cracked ice on sleeping seeds
Frosty breath shiver-shudders words
Waiting.

Spring air
Fairy-wing breeze
Lifting blossom petals
Weightless whispering of summer
Stirring.

Summer
Claiming a crown
Exploding wild colours
In a frenzy of patterning
Clapping.

Coral Rumble

There's a Place

There's a place behind my face
Where no one goes but me
A special space inside my head
That only I can see.

You cannot travel there by car
It's far too far away,
It is a perfect paradise
Where words and pictures play.

And that is where I like to hide
And where I want to be,
Inside my secret island
Where no one can follow me.

Jeanne Willis

Magnificat

My neighbour's been taken to hospital
Asked me to look after his cat
Two helpings of gourmet rabbit per day
She seems contented with that.

I leave the radio switched on for her
To keep her company
She was listening to Desert Island Discs
Last night as I took in her tea.

She's learned how to switch the programmes
She likes the Third Programme best
As superior classical music
Seems to help her to digest.

She sings loudly along with Pavarotti
She thinks Mozart is a lark
Is addicted to Khachaturian
But covers her ears to Bach.

I've told her her master's home next week
She's not happy on the whole
It means goodbye to Chopin and Brahms
And Hello Rock 'n' Roll.

Gareth Owen

Here's What They Are

A Meter Bay –
A Parking Space.

A Teacher's Desk –
A Marking Place.

The Park, for Dogs –
A Barking Space.

The Deep Blue Sea –
A Sharking Place.

Mount Ararat –
An Arking Space.

The Slides and Swings –
A Larking Place.

And deep Black Holes –
A 'Dark' in Space!

Trevor Harvey

Batgirl's Disgrace

Auntie Betty pulls her cloak on
And the mask – the one with ears
Then she flies out of the classroom
Fighting back a flood of tears
All the teachers in the playground
Wag their fingers at the girl
If only she had done her homework
FIRST, before she saved the world

Need calamity prevention?
Sorry, Batgirl's in detention.

Andrea Shavick

The Black Cat

The black cat was fond of fairies.
He liked the gloss of their wings
And the way they darted across the lawn.

At first, he watched them secretly,
Through glass,
And from the middle of a thorn bush,
But when they waved at him
He crept closer, closer
Until they would rest on his paws
Or gather soft handfuls of his fur
With spiky combs.

His golden eyes reflected
The sparks of their wands,
And he only showed his fangs
To other cats,
And the skinny fox.

In his dreams
He did not fly,
Or cast spells over mice
And magpies.
But sometimes he danced
In moonlit circles
With the Fairy Queen.

Clare Bevan

The Bubble Between
Two Buildings

Wet petals stick ragged pink splodges
on to the path
                    that twists and wriggles
under my feet like a long black snake.

The wind is warm, I can smell
blossom as it bends on its branches
watch it fly
                    in a shower of flowers
scattered into the rain spattering down.

I'm stuck in a bubble between two buildings
my arms full of registers, messages, parcels
all the classrooms
                    buzz like beehives full of bustle
children and grown-ups all painting and writing
talking and thinking, laughing and singing
chattering, shouting, counting and weighing.

Outside I can hear
the milk float droning down our street
the other side of the fence
                    two dogs barking
and birds singing in the hedge by the path.

It's still and calm
breathing the blossom-heavy air
I lean into the warm, wet wind
                    wait for my feet
to lead me back to my busy classroom
down the shining tarmac painted with blossom.

David Harmer

River Don

How fortunate is Don
to have a river named after him.
I wish I had something
named after me.
River Brian doesn't sound quite right,
nor does Brian Street or Brian Road.
(There was a Brian Close once
But he was a cricketer.)
Scotland does interesting things with names.
I'd love to be the Pass of Brian
Or the Bridge of Brian – that sounds good.
The name Brian means strength,
tough as cowhide, strong as iron.
Maybe I could be the Mountain of Brian.
If I wanted it to reflect the very core of me,
the very heart, if I wanted it to conjure up
the very Brian-ness of Brian,
I'd find the River Brian flowing in my veins,
Fortress Brian in the heart of me,
Church of Brian in my soul.
And in my eyes, The Great Fire of Brian,
to be glimpsed by everyone
and admired!

Brian Moses

Views of
the Mountain
of Brian

Easter Monday

We tied the white eggs in onion skin,
Wrapped them round with string.
We boiled them for so long
The water looked like strong tea.
Lifted out, the string was a dirty khaki,
But the eggs – the eggs were glorious
Marbled brown, amber and yellow.

When we were at the top of the hill,
When the others rolled theirs down to crack,
I held mine back –
It was too beautiful.

Catherine Benson

Tiger Eyes

Always, always, where she walked,
one left, one right, two tigers stalked.
Sleek and striped, they paced along,
bright and beautiful and strong.
The great heads swung, the wild eyes glowed,
she never feared the lonely road,
the jostling crowd, the bully's sneer
for she had tigers, always near.
As she walked, the grimy streets
echoed to their tiger feet,
slowly padding, menace filled,
prowling past where rubbish spilled,
where shops were closed and graffiti
replaced the flowers, grass and trees.
When jeered at by the local louts
she knew neither fear nor doubt
though most of them were twice her size.
She fixed them with her tiger eyes
and went unharmed, for as they stared,
they almost saw the tigers there,

a gleam of gold, a scrape of claw
a hint, a whisper of a roar,
a shadow cast where no sun shone
an image, fleeting, flickering, gone.
For always, always, as she walked,
one left, one right, two tigers stalked.

Marian Swinger

Read Me

A Poem for Every Day of the Year

READ ME contains a poem for every day of the year from the very best classic and modern poets.

Praise for READ ME

'This book contains Emily Dickinson, Wordsworth, Gareth Owen, Ian McMillan, Wes Magee, William Blake and Seamus Heaney – an excellent acknowledgement of the fact that some days we feel wordy and broody, and on other days we feel as brash as the wind, and no deeper than the surface of our skins. This anthology shows some respect for those changeable habits.'
Michael Glover, *Independent on Sunday*

'Great riches are to be found between the covers of this unassuming paperback . . . this treasure trove celebrates the variety of English verse.'
Beverley Davies, The Lady

'The poetic calendar chosen by Gaby Morgan is a delight: motley, wide-ranging and unpatronising.'
Observer

SENSATIONAL!

Poems inspired by the five senses, chosen by Roger McGough

SENSATIONAL! is a stunning collection of poems inspired by the five senses, chosen by Roger McGough.

In life you can't move without experiencing something sensory – whatever you are doing you will be seeing or smelling or touching or hearing or tasting, and this book has poems about all these things. There are poems about eyes, ears, noses, mouths and hands, and there are even poems that combine them all. Life is a glorious sensational whirl and nowhere is it distilled as effectively as in poetry. Prepare to be dazzled.

Includes poems by the very best classic and contemporary poets, including Carol Ann Duffy, Ian McMillan, John Hegley, Langston Hughes, William Wordsworth, Vernon Scannell and Michael Rosen.